COWARDS

THE TRUE STORY OF THE MEN WHO REFUSED TO FIGHT

MARCUS SEDGWICK

ed

This edition published by Hodder Children's Books 2003

Text copyright © Marcus Sedgwick 2003

Book design by Fiona Webb

Cover illustration by Andy Bridge

10 9 8 7 6 5 4 3 2 1

A catalogue record for this book is available from the British Library.

ISBN: 0 340 86061 8

Printed by Bookmarque Ltd, Croydon, Surrey
Hodder Children's Books
a division of Hodder Headline Limited
338 Euston Road
London NW1 3BH

Contents

Dedication

For my father and grandfather

Acknowledgements

My thanks go to Felicity Goodall for her generous advice, the staff of the Imperial War Museum, in particular Rosemary Tudge, for their assistance, and Anne Clark, for giving me the chance to tell this story.

Author's note

I've wanted to write something about conscientious objectors for a long time. The research for this book started out as research for a novel, but this story is as remarkable as any fictional account could be, and I am glad now that it is a true story that I am telling. I have tried to bring an open mind to this subject, and tell events as they happened as far as I can tell, but I must declare the origin of my interest in the subject. My father and my mother's father were both conscientious objectors, and they fought for what they believed in. This book is dedicated to them.

Introduction

Cowards. The title of this book is deliberately provocative. It is called this to approach head-on the view held by many people about conscientious objectors, both now and in the past.

Conscientious objection is not talked about very much. Not only is it rarely discussed, but when it is, it is unlikely to be discussed in favourable terms. The view that it is at best foolishness, and at worst cowardice, is nearly as common today as it was at the time of the first cases – during the First World War, the period which this book considers.

It has never been 'cool' – pacifism does not generally appeal to young men in the way the image of a gun-toting soldier can. Whatever else you think about it, one question therefore becomes dominant – why on earth does someone go against the opinion of the vast majority of people? What drives them to make a stand they will have to defend in the face of great opposition, abuse and even physical punishment?

The answer is always a personal one, and there are as many reasons as there are conscientious objectors, but belief – the belief that it is wrong to kill – is common to them all. Having had the chance to talk to a few men who were conscientious objectors in the Second World War, the same phrase seems to crop up again and again: 'It was just something I felt I had to do.'

In the Second World War, men like my father and grandfather had to appear before tribunals and make a case to show the genuine nature of their objection to war making. They were able to do this largely as a result of the actions of men in the First World War, men like Howard Marten and Alfred Evans, whose stories are told here. Whatever you think about the rights and wrongs of conscientious objection, I hope that when you have read this book you will believe that these men, and others like them, were certainly not cowards.

CHAPTER 1

OH, WHAT
A LOVELY WAR

MAY 1916. A sealed train speeds through
the night along a carefully selected
route around the outskirts of London. The
train stops at no stations, picks up no more
passengers.

The men on this train are prisoners.

As it passes without stopping through
another dark, wartime station, something is
thrown out onto the platform. It is a note,

hastily written, saying where the men are being sent.

The train has come from Felixstowe, on the east coast of England, and is headed for the port at Southampton. The ultimate destination for the prisoners on the train is France, and the front line of a war that seems to have got nowhere. There are seventeen men aboard the train. They come from a variety of backgrounds, from different jobs, from various parts of the country; but they have one thing in common. They are all conscientious objectors.

One of the men is Alfred Evans. At twenty years of age he is the youngest aboard. Until a few weeks before he had been an apprentice piano tuner. Another, the eldest – but still short of his thirtieth birthday – is Howard Marten, who had been working in a bank.

In a few short months, the lives of these men would be shattered by an incredible ordeal.

Alfred, Howard and the other men on the train have all, for one reason or another, refused to join the army. Though they have now been forcibly conscripted, and are legally and technically soldiers, they still refuse to fight; indeed they refuse to obey any military order. Why? Each of them believes very strongly that it is wrong to kill, even in time of war.

This belief at first seems simple, but for the men on the train it would be sorely tested over the coming months. They would discover just how complicated a belief it is to hold.

Britain entered the First World War on 4th August 1914. It can be hard for us today to understand the attitude of most people at the time to this war. Nowadays we have become used to seeing the events of war as they happen, sometimes literally. The combination of journalists in the heart of a war zone and satellite broadcasting means we often know what is taking place as soon as some of the people actually there. But this is a recent phenomenon. The Vietnam War is often said to have been the first televised war. Some events in the Second World War were filmed, and a very edited version shown in cinemas back home, but at the time of the First World War, the average person had very little real news to go on.

This was a time before television, even before radio was commonplace. Most homes were without electricity, and the motor car was a rare sight. Newspapers were the main form of information, and they could be very out of date, and quite inaccurate.

The way we now view World War One, 'The Great War', is very different to how it was seen at the time.

In Britain, the arrival of war was celebrated almost universally. Ministers were cheered by crowds as they left Parliament after the Declaration of War. Patriotic songs were sung in the streets, and young men were encouraged to join the army, or 'enlist': many did so with enthusiasm. It was seen as an honourable thing for a man to do, as perhaps it still is today, but there was a greater fervour and clamour attached.

Robert Graves, a famous poet who joined the army, described in his autobiography, *Goodbye to All That*, how he found many men in his Company who were either too old or too young to enlist, and who had lied about their age to get to France. He remembers one boy of fifteen, who was discovered and sent back to base. The boy enlisted legally at the age of seventeen, and was killed the same summer.

This celebration of a war is strange to us, as we look back from the beginning of a new century. It is even difficult to understand why the war started in the first place.

Its origins lay in the complicated history of the struggles between various European powers, but very few ordinary people knew much about this: they were just excited by the prospect of a glorious victory.

The war kicked off with a loud hurrah. It was a firmly held view that 'it would all be over by Christmas', a phrase that has since passed into history as a reminder of the folly that this war became. At the outbreak of fighting, leaders on all sides were convinced of swift victories and a rapid end to the war. However, they were to be proved wrong. As early as September 1914 the progress of the war became bogged down in the horrors of trench warfare, in France.

The life of an ordinary soldier in the trenches of the First World War was unbelievably horrific at times, though there were long periods of stalemate and inactivity that resulted in terrible boredom, too. During these periods, which actually amounted to the majority of a soldier's time at the front, the enemies they struggled with were rats and lice, too little – and bad – food, and illness. Rats overran the trenches at times, scavenging what they could, picking over the remains of fallen soldiers abandoned in no-man's land. They were bold animals, not easily scared away even with a well-aimed boot. But the lice were worse. All of a soldier's uniform quickly became infested with the tiny crawling pests, so that the wearer might scratch himself raw. Soldiers soon learnt tricks to get rid of the lice: they were most persistent along the seams of clothing, so you would try and kill them by running a fingernail or a match or lighter flame along the seams. Once a company was relieved from the trenches, it would retire to a

French village a mile or two behind the front, where the men might have their first bath in weeks. While they scrubbed themselves free of lice, their clothes would be disinfected and for a few hours the soldiers would be rid of the problem. However, very soon, the warmth of the men's bodies would hatch the tiny eggs that had lain undisturbed despite the disinfection process, and a new army of lice would begin to drive the men crazy again.

While behind the lines, the men might also get some decent food, but at the front it was very different. The food was terrible and in short supply. Even the tea tasted of petrol as water was often carried to the front in old fuel cans.

In the history of trench life there are strange tales – like how men would boil the water for their tea by placing a metal mug on top of a Lewis machine gun and then firing a thousand rounds or so into no-man's land, so that the heat from the bullets being fired would warm up the water.

The boredom and tension of waiting, on edge, for the next attack to begin was a terrible mixture that was almost as bad as an attack itself.

But not quite.

We are now able to read full accounts – by the men who were there – of the horrors of the war; but at the time their true situation was unknown to those back home.

Before an attack, which usually happened at night, each side would try and weaken the enemy by bombarding them for hours, sometimes even days, with large calibre shells. Many men were killed directly in the trenches by these shells. There were many cases where men were killed by shells fired by their own side falling short onto their own lines. Then the huge guns would suddenly cease, and the men would have to go 'over the top' to attempt to capture the enemy trench. Many would not even get fully up and out of their own trench before they were cut down by machine-gun fire. Those who survived might manage to stagger a few yards into no-man's land before being killed or wounded. If wounded, a man would probably die where he lay – for the most part it was too dangerous to try and recover men stranded in this way.

The following lines of poetry are written from the point of view of an officer, reflecting on the men under his command.

My men go wearily with their monstrous
*   burdens,*
they bear wooden planks and iron sheeting
*   through the area of death.*
When a flare curves through the sky, they
*   rest, immobile.*
Then on again, swearing and blaspheming.

A man of mine lies on the wire.
It is death to fetch his soulless corpse.
A man of mine lies on the wire.
And he will rot, and first his lips the worms
*   will eat.*
It is not thus I would have him kissed.

The sunny days of August had turned into heavy, persistent rains. Stalemate was soon to follow. Warfare had changed: new weapons like the machine-gun were proving crucial, but British High Command still believed that the war would be won with cavalry, like wars of the previous century. The German forces, meanwhile, had concentrated on building up defensive positions along the front lines, with machine-gun posts in concrete bunkers. As a result, many British and French attacks were doomed to end in slaughter. Losses were high. In the Battle of Neuve Chapelle, in Spring 1915, the British General Haig ordered that his men should attempt an advance. He considered this to be the most 'soldierly' way out of the stalemate. At the beginning of the battle nearly a thousand soldiers were killed attempting to cut enemy wire in one sector alone. Haig ordered the battle to continue regardless of the loss of life. By mid-March about 12,000 men had died.

They had gained less than a mile of ground.

In *Goodbye to All That* Robert Graves tells the story of a company commander named Captain Furber, whose nerves were in pieces. He made a bet with another officer that the trenches in his sector of the front line wouldn't have moved more than a mile in another two years. Everyone laughed at Captain Furber, but he won the bet.

The army was undeterred, however. When warned that there would be continual heavy losses at Ypres, later in 1915, General Allenby remarked, 'What the hell does that matter? There are plenty more men in England.'

The problem was getting them. Battles like Ypres and Neuve Chappelle were creating heavy losses of life. The army was eating soldiers almost as fast as it could give them three weeks' basic training, and it was running short of men.

The military put pressure on the government to provide a solution, and they did. An Act was passed that would change things forever.

For the first time in history, British men were subject to conscription: they were compelled to join the army whether they wanted to or not.

It is here that the war catches up with men like Howard Marten and Alfred Evans, for these men were conscientious objectors, and would refuse to fight, even until the point where they faced death themselves.

Much would still happen before they found themselves aboard that sealed train heading for the coast. They faced horrors both at home and abroad, but that moment on the train would prove crucial.

No one now recalls who threw the note onto that deserted platform, but the act threw a precious lifeline to all seventeen men aboard.

CHAPTER 2

WHITE FEATHER

A LFRED EVANS, a Londoner, is an apprentice in a piano factory. A quick-witted young man, and always ready with a joke, he is also highly philosophical at times. Howard Marten, also from London, is a bank clerk. Quieter than Alfred, and almost always serious, he not only has a strong sense of justice, but also the independent nature of an only child. He has close-cropped hair, and behind his round spectacles, a pair of piercing eyes.

These men are just two of around 16,500 men who claimed a conscientious objection to fighting in the First World War. Their stories are typical of the experiences of many of these men, although they are exceptional in some ways.

Their belief that it is wrong to kill under any circumstance, was very unusual at the time. As a result, conscientious objectors were scorned, reviled or insulted by almost every other member of society. Once word got around that a man was a conscientious objector, verbal abuse was common, with both strangers and acquaintances calling them 'coward', or worse. The word 'conchie' – short for conscientious objector – became a term of abuse, and many were stopped in the street and handed a white feather – the sign of cowardice.

They received not just verbal, but physical abuse, too. Alfred and Howard, along with the other fifteen men on the train, would later even face death itself.

Many conscientious objectors seem to have been able to draw strength from the hostility they faced.

Howard was one of these.

'I remember telling somebody that if I was the only person in this world I would take this attitude. That's how I felt about it. It was a very personal thing.'

Alfred Evans, like many who chose to register an objection to war, found himself the target of hostility not only from members of the public, but from members of his own family, too. An aunt who came to see him made it clear she disapproved of his standpoint, telling him to 'stop all this nonsense'. She offered him some money and told him to stop making a fool of himself. Things were bad for him at work too. Once war broke out and it became known that Alfred was a pacifist, the men he worked with at the piano factory wouldn't speak to him. He even had the same experience at church: when leaving after Mass, other churchgoers spat on the floor in front of him.

Howard had an easier time from his friends and family since many of them were Quakers, and like him, held the view that all forms of violence were wrong.

There were many reasons why men held pacifist beliefs, but there seem to have been two main philosophies.

The early part of the last century was a time of great political activity. Socialism was a strong movement, which argued that the working classes were exploited by the ruling elite – the government, employers, the wealthy.

Alfred Evans came from a family that was
politically aware. His father was an active
trade union member and was president of his
branch of the United Kingdom Society of
Coachmakers. He did this despite the fact that
if his employers had found out he would have
been sacked. Alfred recalls how his family
would argue points of politics or philosophy
at the dinner table, letting their meal go cold
while they settled a point.

Alfred had one particularly significant
conversation with his father. It was in 1910,
and at Tonypandy in Wales the coal-miners
had gone on strike for better wages. Winston
Churchill, who would go on to be Prime
Minister in the Second World War, was then
the Home Secretary. He had ordered troops
down to Tonypandy. Shots were fired in other
industrial disputes at the time, too. Alfred
remembers what his father said to him.

'If I strike for a reasonable living for you and your father, then if you become a soldier, it will be your business to shoot me down.'

This quote captures the essence of the Socialist opposition to the war. Socialists believed in a brotherhood of the common man that transcended national boundaries. Their allies were not the ruling classes in their own country, but their fellow workers in any country, even a country their government was at war with. They believed that the First World War was an unnecessary war, made by European rulers to further their own ends, using the working masses as cannon fodder.

Alfred Evans also had a religious belief, which increased his objection to war. Religious conviction formed the basis of the other main strand of objection. Howard

Marten is an example of this type of objector. He came from a family with a pacifist background; his father was a Quaker, the common name for a member of the Society of Friends. The Quaker faith is essentially a Christian movement, with no written creed or ordained ministers and with strong pacifist beliefs.

Howard remembers the views he held, even as a young schoolboy.

'I was as a boy always inclined to pacifist views. I could never side with the idea of martial violence. I felt that that was inconsistent with our Christian beliefs.'

Even during first years of the war, before conscription was introduced, Alfred and Howard knew they were facing difficult times. Despite the enthusiasm of most of the country for the war, there was not widespread support for conscription, but it was obvious to many that the military and the government were working towards it.

In July 1915, the National Registration Act was introduced. When it came into force in August, every man between sixteen and forty was compelled to register as a citizen. The government denied that this was intended to ease the possible introduction of conscription, but many pacifists were not convinced. Losses were still running high: in addition to the mass slaughter of the attack and counter-attack in the trenches, there was also combat in the air and even underground in tunnels dug to undermine the enemy's trenches. 1915 saw the introduction of chlorine gas as a weapon, soon to be followed by other chemical agents that would further increase loss of life.

The army needed more men and the government would have to find them.

The next idea was the Derby Scheme, under which men were asked to 'attest', which meant they agreed to serve in the army when called. The government played some clever games at this time. They promised married men that they would not call them up until the supply of all single men had been used up. Many married men happily joined under the Derby Scheme, convinced they would probably never be called up. It wasn't long before many of them were.

Around this time, a group called the No-Conscription Fellowship was founded, with the purpose of monitoring and supporting those who chose to express their pacifist beliefs in the face of conscription. This organisation was vital in the struggle of conscientious objectors against the military, and would play a vital part in Alfred and Howard's story too.

Howard became Chairman of the Harrow branch of the No-Conscription Fellowship, and remembers that he had to consider the implications of his beliefs even before conscription was introduced.

'I never had two minds about my personal position in the event of conscription...we had to face, even at that stage, how far our views were consistent with an extreme attitude: that is, were we prepared to adopt a pacifist position even to the point of being shot?

We little realized at the time that it would come to that.'

It is one thing to hold a view or a belief like this in theory, but it is another to continue to hold it when put to the test. For Howard and Alfred, it would prove to be a very extreme test indeed.

CHAPTER 3

A HARD PATH

O<small>N</small> 2<small>ND</small> M<small>ARCH</small> 1916, eighteen months after the start of the war, the Military Service Act – as it was known – came into force.

The pressure on young men had been building steadily through the early part of the war. As more and more men went to France and never returned, or came back mutilated, those that remained were seen as shirkers, or cowards.

Poster campaigns were run by the
Parliamentary Recruiting Service, featuring
now famous slogans such as: 'Daddy, what
did YOU do in the Great War?' underneath
a picture of a small girl sitting on her father's
lap; 'Women of Britain say – GO!';
'Britons – your country needs you', and then,
shortly before the Military Service Act,
'Will you march, too, or wait until
March 2?'

After the Military Service Act came into
force, every unmarried man in the country
between the ages of eighteen and 41 was
deemed to have enlisted in the army.

Alfred and Howard received their call-up
papers but failed to respond to them. As a
result they would have received a visit from
a policeman, and then appeared before a
tribunal, a kind of local court established by
the government.

The purpose of these tribunals was to hear men's cases for claiming exemption from military service on various grounds, including conscientious objection for religious or moral reasons. They were empowered to grant absolute exemption, or to hand out 'non-combatant service', which meant the objector would have to accept work that was outside the regular army but still deemed to be of 'national importance'. The nature of such work could be anything from farming or mining, to medical work, to making ammunition.

The tribunals were newly established bodies, composed of local notable figures and tradesmen, members of the church and the army. They were given guidelines by which to work, but what actually went on in them varied greatly. The tribunal in Liverpool was known to be extremely vindictive; the one in Manchester reasonably impartial.

Howard remembers the men on his tribunal board:

> *'The local tribunal was pretty hostile. They were men of not very great depth of vision or understanding.'*

There are countless cases of tribunals acting in a manner that, at best, can be described as bullying, and at worst, illegal. Here are just a few of them.

At Leyton, in London, the tribunal members told a man they had no power to grant absolute exemption, when they not only did have the power, but had actually granted someone else exemption only six days before.

At Seaton Delaval in Northumberland, the chairman told a man that if he refused non-combatant service he would be shot. Likewise, in Sheffield, a man was told the only way to achieve absolute exemption was through death. At Wigton in Cumbria, a man who was dumb appeared before the tribunal. His father was present to speak for him, but was not allowed to do so, and the man's case was dismissed.

At Tipton in the West Midlands a man who was physically disabled and unable to appear due to his health, sent his statement to the tribunal via a friend. The board announced, illegally, that it was 'not allowed'.

At Springhead, near Oldham, two brothers were due to appear before the tribunal. The appeal of the first was heard, and dismissed. The board refused to hear the second brother's case on the grounds that it was a 'waste of time'.

Another man, at Bermondsey in London, objected that one of the members of the tribunal board was reading a newspaper during his trial. He was told, 'You protest,

do you? Well, you can go on protesting.'
The newspaper reader automatically held up
his hand at the end of the case, dismissing
the applicant without even having listened to
his case.

At another tribunal in Oxford a man was
refused when he admitted that he was a
Socialist.

At Oldbury, in the Midlands, a member of
the tribunal asked the applicant, 'Do you
really mean to say you wouldn't kill
anybody?' When the applicant confirmed this,
his questioner replied, 'What an awful state of
mind to be in!'

A Christian objector at Worcester, again in
the Midlands, was told, 'But the very essence
of Christianity is fighting. The Old Testament
is full of it.'

It seems that again and again the tribunals
simply did not believe that the men claiming a
conscientious objection to fighting were

anything other than cowards, out to save
themselves.

Tribunals had favourite questions they used,
to try and pick holes in a claimant's objection.
One of these, for example, was, 'What would
you do if a German was attacking your sister
(or mother)?' Any answer that involved
aggression would lay the claimant open to a
charge of hypocrisy: if a man would fight to
protect his family, why would he not fight to
protect his countrymen? One defendant said,
'I would endeavour to interpose myself
between them.' Another, 'I would try and
make terms with him.'
Others carefully outlined the difference
between an individual struggle and the
organised warfare of nation against nation.
But conscientious objectors often struggled to
answer this difficult question satisfactorily
and their cases were dismissed as a result.

Some of the exemptions that *were* given by
various tribunals are just as strange as some
of the reasons why applications were refused.
For example, one man was given exemption
because he had provided wine for some
troops, as were all the brewers of the
Brentford Brewery Company. All men
employed in fox hunting were given
exemption, on the grounds that their work
was of national importance.

Alfred and Howard appeared before their
tribunals in March 1916. Like all the 16,500
conscientious objectors in the war they faced
a panel of local 'dignitaries' – frequently
elderly businessmen or churchmen. There
were very few women, and only in the
tribunals in the largest towns were you likely
to find a magistrate or judge, or anyone with
any legal experience. The sessions took place
in local courts and other halls and all were

supposed to be open to the public, though
many frequently flouted this aspect of the law,
conducting their business behind closed doors.

There was a division amongst conscientious
objectors over the question of what type of
work they could accept. Some felt that to
accept any military work was unacceptable.
Alfred was not among these at the time of his
tribunal, though later events made him change
his mind.

At his tribunal he stated that he was
prepared to work for the Royal Army Medical
Corps, which tended wounded soldiers at and
behind the front lines. He was given a fair
hearing and granted an exemption certificate
by the tribunal. As it turned out, however, a
career with the Medical Corps was not what
lay in store for Alfred.

On 25th April, he reported at the recruiting
office in Ealing. The officer he spoke to asked

for his exemption certificate. When Alfred handed it over, the man tore it up in front of him. He then put a new document on the table, telling Alfred that he was to join the Non-Combatant Corps, and that he was to sign the paper in front of him, without even reading it.

Alfred refused. The officer immediately called a corporal and two other men, and Alfred was taken away under armed guard to Hounslow Barracks. He felt confused by all this, and unsure what he should do. He decided to await further events, which might help him decide his future conduct.

Howard was of a different mindset. Although he wasn't a complete 'absolutist', as some objectors were known, he felt unable to follow any military orders. As a result his tribunal rejected his claim. After his appearance at a magistrate's court he was told to wait for a military escort, which took him away to Mill Hill Barracks.

For both Alfred and Howard, the stakes were becoming more serious. It wouldn't be long before they met, in very unpleasant circumstances.

CHAPTER 4

ALONE NO MORE

BY APRIL 1916 Howard and Alfred found themselves in the hands of the military. Almost immediately, Howard realized there were decisions to be made. The first thing the army wanted him, and all the conscientious objectors, to do was to put on a uniform. Howard was unhappy about this, but understood that the soldiers in charge of him had orders to dress him in a uniform, if necessary by force. Howard never believed in making his protests with force. He agreed to put on the uniform, under protest, saying it wouldn't alter his attitude.

'When it came to the crunch, it's what you would do, not what you would wear, that was much more important. And you can't be compelled to do certain things against your will.'

Howard was sent to an army camp called Landguard at Felixstowe, on the Suffolk coast.

Other conscientious objectors tried to resist having a uniform put on them. Two sergeants wrestled Howard Blake into his trousers, with much abuse and force. Then the men realized they'd been trying to put both his legs into one trouser leg, and they all laughed. The rest of the process was finished in a friendlier manner, and they shook hands at the end.

George Dutch, a Quaker, was not so lucky. When told that he refused to put on uniform, the major in charge of the camp where he was being held took extreme action. Saying that in his opinion conscientious objection was just another name for outright cowardice, he ordered that George should be stripped, and left in a tent high on a cliff overlooking the sea. It was cold, misty weather. The sides of the tents were rolled up and he was left to freeze, or put the uniform on. He sat in just his underwear in the tent for over ten days and nights. Finally the camp doctor intervened in his case.

Alfred met with a piece of luck. He had been passed fit for active service at the barracks in Hounslow. He stated again that he was still prepared to join the Royal Army Medical Corps, but the colonel of the camp told him he could do nothing about it.

He was to be sent to Landguard Camp at Felixstowe, but the colonel told him he could go without escort, provided he gave his word that he would not try and escape. Alfred did so, and this gave him the opportunity to contact his family, as well as the No-Conscription Fellowship.

True to his word, Alfred boarded the train for Felixstowe in good faith, but, alarmingly, arrived in the middle of a Zeppelin raid. London and the east coast of Britain were prone to attack by these early airships, which dropped primitive but destructive incendiary bombs onto cities below. Although Zeppelins were huge lumbering aircraft, which could often be easily shot down, they formed the first airborne attack on Great Britain, and were greatly feared as a result.

Upon arrival at Landguard Camp, Alfred was put into a hut holding twenty or so Non-Combatant Corps men. These were other men who had tried to gain exemption from conscription for various reasons, but whose applications had been refused. They told him that they were being treated well, that things were easy for them.

Alfred was not impressed. Men in the Non-Combatant Corps worked for the army, and engaged in many tasks to assist soldiers. Many conscientious objectors, Alfred among them, found this attitude difficult to accept. Typical of his plain-speaking manner, he told them he had no intention of joining the Non-Combatant Corps.

> *'I let them understand that I thought nothing of a man who carried shells and arms in general, for other men to fight.'*

Alfred, unsurprisingly, was insulted by men in the hut, despite the fact that they had all attempted to avoid military service themselves.

It was this hypocrisy that Alfred took
objection to; in fact he had every respect for
a soldier who believed in what he was doing.
He once said, 'If you believe in being a soldier
then you should be one.'

The next day, Alfred refused to obey any
orders, and was taken before the officer in
charge of the camp, Major Greenfield. Alfred
remembers him as a reasonable man, and he
again asked to join the Royal Army Medical
Corps. The major said he was unable to make
any such decision. Alfred was sent back to
join the other Non-Combatant Corps men, on
'fatigue' duty, peeling potatoes. Alfred had no
objection to doing the work, but still found
himself unable to obey any military order.

The corporal in charge reported him at once
to a sergeant, and it wasn't long before he
was back in front of Major Greenfield, who
was not so friendly this time. Alfred was

sentenced to 28 days' Field Punishment
Number One.

Field Punishment Number One was the
most severe sentence the army could hand
out, short of the death penalty. What it
actually involved in practice could vary
greatly. It had originated as a punishment on
the battlefield itself: the offender would be
tied to the side of the huge wheels of a gun
carriage whilst it was in action. The prisoner
would then at the very least be thrown and
battered by the powerful recoil of the gun, to
say nothing of the dangers posed by the enemy.

Alfred was marched off to the guardroom,
and it was there that he met Howard Marten
for the first time, along with fifteen other
conscientious objectors who were also
refusing to do Non-Combatant Corps work.

Two days later, the men were told how they
would serve their 28 days' punishment.

Felixstowe sits at the tip of the southern side of the River Stour. They were across the river to the town of Harwich, with its old fortress dating from the time of the Napoleonic Wars.

The Harwich Circular Redoubt.

CHAPTER 5

IN THE DARK

HARWICH REDOUBT is an oppressive place even today. It was built between 1806 and 1810, during the threat of invasion by the French under Napoleon. It is a massive concrete structure with three feet thick walls, shaped like a doughnut, 60 metres across. The centre of the ring is a circular parade ground 25 metres across.

The redoubt was never needed for its original purpose of keeping the French out of England, and by the 1900s was being used as barrack accommodation. During the First World War it became a military prison.

It was here that the seventeen conscientious objectors from Landguard Camp at Felixstowe were sent, in April 1916.

Alfred would never forget his time there: 'It was a vile place, in which severe punishment was given out.'

Very quickly the men found themselves in trouble. Sticking to their decision not to obey any military orders, they refused to take part in drill.

Howard was one of five men who were then handcuffed and made to stand with their faces to the wall of the parade ground.

After they had been standing there for some time, a friendly cat came along, and persistently rubbed itself against the prisoners' legs. Howard heard the man to his right whisper to the cat, 'Why, pussy, you're the only Christian in this place!'

This punishment was just a taster of
things to come: a sergeant, a huge man with
a huge voice, warned them that if they
continued to refuse to drill, they would face
much worse.

But refuse they did, and the next day they
were given three days 'cells'. This meant
solitary confinement in the punishment cells,
on a diet of biscuits and water.

The punishment cells were built end-to-end,
three in a row, into the hillside. The only
light to reach the second cell came through a
filthy window in the wall between it and the
first. Likewise, the only light reaching the
innermost cell came from number two. It
never grew light enough in the third cell to be
able to see well enough to read, and even the
outermost cell was a gloomy place.

At night the cells were very cold. Even
during the day, when their blankets and
overcoats would be taken from them, it was

impossible to get warm. There was no furniture of any kind, except a metal sheet set into the wall to serve as a small table.

Alfred recalls the horror of the punishment cells. Almost completely dark, the walls ran with water, and they were visited frequently by rats. The prisoners were allowed out only once a day briefly, to wash, and were allowed no exercise.

They were given a total of eight dry biscuits a day to eat, and a little water.

During his time in solitary confinement, Howard kept himself going by walking up and down in the darkness of the cell. He would picture himself walking along a busy road in town, or along a country lane.

On their first Sunday in the redoubt, the men were released before midday, and gathered in one of the dormitories. Howard found the occasion one of great value:

'We *must have presented a quaint
spectacle, arrayed in our khaki uniforms,
and seated in a circle on kit bags,
mattresses and overcoats. Such times of
fellowship were occasions of deep
spiritual experience.*'

Now they had a chance to talk, Alfred and
Howard and the others discussed their
situation avidly. It was clearly the army's
intention to get these men to become soldiers.
The officers seemed determined to break their
will with threats, abuse and physical
punishments; but these methods only served
to reinforce the men's beliefs.

However, they found it difficult to work
out some of the details of their objections to
military service. They were normal men, and
perfectly happy to work, but only if it was
not military work. Howard wrestled with
these questions. Exactly what type of work

was military? Was it just plain stupid to refuse to help with anything?

In the end, they decided to agree to do purely domestic work in the redoubt, but to continue to refuse to drill.

For a while they also agreed to do some work outside the fort, and were put to work carting stones from the beach. Then they found out that the stones were to make a road to a military camp, and refused to help any further.

Instead they were ordered to do a variety of nonsensical tasks, such as scrubbing the flagstones of the courtyard on their hands and knees, when using a mop would have been quicker and more effective. They had to try and empty the well in the centre of the parade ring with an old pail. They might have been at this forever, had the rusty old chain holding the bucket not broken, sending the bucket crashing down the well.

They also did domestic work around the fort, as they had agreed. Howard liked some of this work, for it meant cleaning up in the officers' mess:

'This might mean a hasty mouthful of tea, or an extra biscuit, and I well remember hugging a marmalade jar and scraping the sides with a grimy finger in order to get a tantalising taste of its former appetising contents.'

However, there were more punishments to come. Alfred and two other men, Rendell Wyatt and Bernard Bonner, were tied up in straightjackets and made to stand against the wall of the parade ground. It was now May, the sun was fierce, and their guards had seen to it that the straps of the straightjackets were pulled too tight. After several hours of this, they were returned to their cells.

Despite their own problems, Howard and the others managed to find sympathy for others in a worse predicament than themselves.

'It was impossible to grow fat upon the diet, and not always easy to laugh over it. We, doing the indoor work, felt famished, and our sympathy went out to the unhappy prisoners who, on this miserable food, were expected to do a day's heavy manual labour, with drill morning and evening, with full marching kit...

Each night, for an hour or two after we retired, the dormitories echoed with volleys of foul language.'

Things were not to stay this way. The military felt it could not allow this disobedience to continue, and had a plan to put a stop to it.

On Saturday 6th May, the men were returned across the estuary to the barracks at Landguard, Felixstowe. Just after they had finished dinner, they were taken in to see Colonel Croft, one by one. As each man came out, the men still waiting could tell that something serious had happened, but with guards present they were unable to talk. At last Alfred's turn came.

He found Colonel Croft surrounded by officers of lesser rank. 'I am sorry to tell you,' said the Colonel, 'that I am instructed by the War Office to cancel the order for your district court martial, and to send you to France with the 2nd Company of the Eastern Non-Combatant Corps.'

Alfred, like the others, was not entirely surprised. Their guards at the redoubt had frequently told them they would soon be 'pushing the daisies up'.

'*An officer told us we were to be taken in irons to France where we should be under active service conditions, and if we persisted in our line of conduct we would be shot.*'

The colonel also told Howard that once they were in France, their 'friends in Parliament' would not be able to help them. All seventeen men were asked to sign the active-service pay book, and take their pay. They refused. They were asked to make their wills. They refused.

Again, the stakes had been raised. Within 36 hours they would be in France.

CHAPTER 6

HELL BOUND

NOW THIS STORY has caught up with itself. After a hasty breakfast the men were put on the train at Felixstowe. It was three o'clock in the morning on 7th May. The train carried not only the seventeen conscientious objectors, but the men of the Non-Combatant Corps as well. It took them around London in a circuitous fashion, and from this and the early start to their journey it was clear to the men that secrecy was part of the army's scheme to deal with them.

Eventually, after a long, slow journey, they reached the port at Southampton. It was now 5.45 in the early evening. Immediately, they were put aboard the *SS Viper*, the ship that would take them to France, painted with camouflage patterns. Within the hour, they set sail.

Once on board the *Viper*, the men were locked in a cabin in the dark; no lights were permitted on the ship above deck. They were given back the few personal things that had been taken from them at Felixstowe. They were told that now they were on a troop ship bound for France they were deemed 'free men', and all their previous offences were to be forgotten.

It was also an army rule that no man should be in handcuffs whilst on board ship, and so their irons were removed from them as well.

They were fed, for the first time since three o'clock that morning, with tea, biscuits and corned beef.

Many of the men were seasick, and due to the horrendous overcrowding on the ship and the darkness in the cabins, it wasn't long before sleeping men had rolled in the mess, and others had trodden it about.

Finally, the men were let out on deck. There was just enough light to see. It was an amazing sight, one that had an impact on Howard.

'Never shall I forget the spectacle of a huddled mass of humanity occupying every available corner of the transport; and a heart-rending sight it was. The circumstances of our own position were forgotten for the moment before the manifestation of the appalling tragedy then being enacted on the battlefields of Flanders.'

The boat was massively overcrowded with young recruits headed for the front line. Howard was taken aback by the scale of the whole affair – this was just one boat of many taking fledgling soldiers to face the horrors of the war raging away relatively few miles inland.

At 6 am the *SS Viper* docked at Le Havre, in France.

The letter thrown from the train onto a platform by one of the Non-Combatant Corps men signifies a critical moment in the men's story. It could have been picked up by anyone, and it might not have been found at all. By chance it was found by someone kind enough to forward it to its destination, and so the men's relatives and the No-Conscription Fellowship got the first word that they were being sent to France.

CHAPTER 7

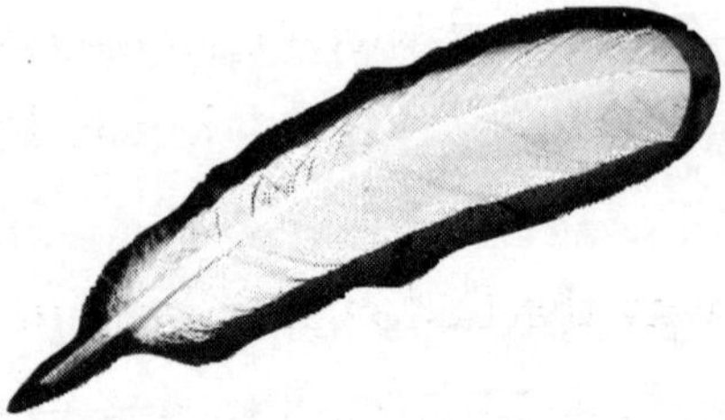

FRIENDS BACK HOME

THE NO-CONSCRIPTION Fellowship had been busy since its formation in early 1915. It was created almost accidentally. Fenner Brockway, the editor of *The Labour Leader* newspaper in Manchester, published a letter he had written at the suggestion of his wife. In it he proposed that all men who would refuse conscription should enrol in a Fellowship. Names poured in in unexpected numbers, Mrs Brockway began to collect them all, and the No-Conscription Fellowship was born.

Right away the Fellowship became a centre of activity and agitation, and just as quickly it found itself in trouble with the law. It was essentially an illegal organisation, and fought running battles with the police and the military.

The No-Conscription Fellowship was a unique organisation, aligned to no particular political views, and relying on no religious belief. Its aims were simple: to support any man who had refused to accept military service.

At its creation it announced the following Statement of Faith.

The No-Conscription Fellowship is an organisation of men likely to be called upon to undertake military service in the

*event of conscription, who will refuse from
conscientious motives to bear arms, because
they consider human life to be sacred, and
cannot, therefore, assume the responsibility
of inflicting death. They deny the right of
Governments to say, 'You shall bear arms,'
and will oppose every effort to introduce
compulsory military service into Great
Britain. Should such efforts be successful,
they will, whatever the consequences may
be, obey their conscientious convictions
rather than the commands of Governments.*

This was their optimistic rallying cry at the
outbreak of war. By 1916 however, things
were not looking so good. Conscription had
been introduced, despite their attempts in
Parliament to prevent it.

In March 1916, when Alfred and Howard
and many others were going to court to state

their objections to war, the No-Conscription Fellowship began to publish its own newspaper, *The Tribunal*. It was only four pages long but, incredibly, had a readership of 100,000. The existence of this newspaper became a considerable annoyance to the government, which did its best to have it shut down. Its offices were raided time and time again, and the editors often arrested, but somehow they always managed to get the next issue out on time.

On 8th April, at the No-Conscription Fellowship convention in Manchester, Fenner Brockway read out the names of the first fifteen men who were in the army's hands.

Things started to get really bad in May, when the prosecution of the entire leadership of the No-Conscription Fellowship began. They were taken to court for publishing a leaflet called *Repeal the Act*. This argued that the Military Service Act, which had brought about conscription, should be overturned. The man responsible for prosecuting the National Committee of the No-Conscription Fellowship was the Crown Advocate, Mr Bodkin. At the trial he made a remarkable statement, saying:

> *'War would become impossible if all men were to have the view that war was wrong.'*

These words could have come from the lips of a conscientious objector. In fact, after the war the slogan 'Wars will cease when men refuse to fight', became a favourite of a new organisation called the Peace Pledge Union.

The No-Conscription Fellowship didn't miss the opportunity to have some fun. They immediately issued a poster containing nothing but Mr Bodkin's words, naming him, the government's own prosecutor, as the source.

The government failed to see the humour of the situation and prosecuted a journalist for displaying the poster. In court, the journalist's lawyer came face to face with Mr Bodkin himself, and had a great time teasing the Crown Advocate. He demanded that Mr Bodkin should be arrested, as the author of the dangerous words. Later, *The Tribunal* offered to support Mr Bodkin's wife and children if he felt it his duty to put himself in prison. But, unamused, the court gave the journalist a fine of £120, or 91 days in prison.

At the end of the trial of the National Committee of the No-Conscription Fellowship eight members were found guilty. They were fined a total of £800, but they decided that five of them should refuse to pay the fines as a protest. These included Fenner Brockway, the Fellowship's Secretary who, with his wife, had started the whole thing.

The five presented themselves to the police
and were imprisoned.

With many of its leaders behind bars, the
responsibility of helping conscientious
objectors fell on new shoulders. Many of
these people were women, like Violet Tillard,
who set up the Fellowship's Maintenance
Organisation, which published the news
sheet that kept all members of the Fellowship
aware of the latest developments. For refusing
to reveal the name of the printers of this
publication, she was herself sent to prison
for 61 days.

Then there was the Information Bureau,
which was also run by women. It kept record
cards for every conscientious objector,
detailing their tribunals, their court cases, and
their current whereabouts. They could pass
this information to the friends and families of
imprisoned men, and it enabled them to keep
up a network of communication between

objectors who would otherwise have been silenced.

These records were incredibly thorough and the government knew it. Many times they tried to find the whereabouts of the Bureau's offices to seize the records, but they never succeeded.

Despite the troubles the No-Conscription Fellowship was facing at home it continued to do all it could to support conscientious objectors, wherever they were. It knew that Alfred, Howard and the other fifteen men from Harwich Redoubt were being sent to France, thanks to the note thrown from the train. The Fellowship tried its utmost to track down the location of the men, but got nowhere for some time. Another piece of good fortune would provide the vital clue, as we shall see in Chapter 9.

There were other organisations that existed to further the cause of peace. One of these was the Society of Friends – the official name of the Quaker movement. At the outbreak of war they circulated a Declaration on the War to all their Meetings, stating that 'all war is utterly incompatible with the plain precepts of our Divine Lord'.

They established several committees to try and alleviate the sufferings caused by war. These included the Friends' Ambulance Unit, which provided ambulance services on the front line, and the War Victims' Relief Committee, which brought food and medicine to civilian victims of the war across France and Belgium.

But it is the No-Conscription Fellowship that has the largest part to play in this story.

CHAPTER 8

INTO THE FIRE

THE *SS VIPER* had docked safely at Le Havre. Alfred, Howard and the others waited while the troops on the ship disembarked. They were then taken off the ship to an army base in Le Havre, Cinder City Camp.

Cinder City Camp was a curious place; an industrial work camp full of men deemed permanently unfit for military service.

The new arrivals were given a chance to clean up, and then they were addressed by a

sergeant from a Scottish regiment, the
Camerons. He was considerate at first, telling
them that all their former crimes were to be
overlooked, and that they had a chance to
make a fresh start. Very soon however, it
became clear that the men did not want to
make any sort of start at all, and continued
their strategy of refusing to obey military
orders.

The seventeen were split up, and each man
sent to work with a different group in the
camp. They refused to work.

During this time, officers came round telling
each man separately that the other sixteen
had given in and had started working. Alfred
found it hard to face this alone, but still
refused to change his mind.

By nightfall he was taken back to the
barracks, where he found the others had not
given in as he had been told. Now the
sergeant, who had been reasonable with

them before, was furious. He hurled abuse at them, as Alfred remembers,

> '*With no rhyme, no rhythm, no even picturesque inventiveness to enliven the proceedings, but plenty of hoarse shouting and venomous abuse.*'

If Alfred was not impressed with the sergeant's unimaginative insults, he was to be very impressed by events the next day.

The army continued to try and break the men's wills by separating them. The entire camp was sent out on parade. There were about twelve companies of around 100 men each, and the seventeen conscientious objectors were split up among this large number of men.

Alfred takes up the story, clearly remembering every detail.

'*On the vast parade ground, before a line
of some 30 officers, were paraded about
1000 men, and one of us was placed with
each battalion or whatever the number was,
and the parade was then ordered to "'shun!
Right turn! Quick march!"'*

The parade moved off, except for seventeen
solitary figures, who stood motionless.

'*Not one of us moved. There was a lot of
shouting and movement amongst the
officers as the mass of men nearly reached
the edge of the parade ground and small
parties were sent back, and we were
dragged off. For a short time it must have
been an amazing sight to see this small
group of us scattered motionless over the
vast parade ground. I'm sure none of us
present will ever forget that sight.*'

Howard knew something special was happening.

'It was unprecedented. The military authorities didn't know quite how to react to it. It was something quite outside their experience. And it became clear that we weren't people that could be bullied.
I think the idea was to break us. They thought that by threatening us in one way or another way they would break the resistance, and that would settle the matter, and of course it didn't. You don't break resistance by threatening people.'

He felt that, like the tribunals they had faced earlier, the army officers believed the objectors to be acting only to save themselves, and that they could not be struggling to uphold a principle.

'They thought we were always out to save our skin; not for a principle. And when they found we were fighting for a principle, they couldn't understand it; it was something right outside their ken.'

After being dragged from the parade ground, the men were marched off to the army service stores. Alfred was sent to an engineering workshop, and was told to feed an automatic saw. He didn't stand to attention before the officer giving the orders, and had his ankles kicked together. The officer left, but Alfred did no work.

A Scottish soldier came over to him and said, 'I don't agree with you, laddy, but I admire your pluck,' and gave Alfred a drink of tea, for which he was very grateful. After a while the officer returned, and there were angry scenes. He was kicked into attention again.

Later that afternoon, Howard and Alfred were put into a foundry, casting metalwork for railway tracks. The sight before them was a grim one: it was hard, hot work in the foundry and the men there were clearly having a bad time. Alfred and Howard felt sorry for them and decided to lend a hand. After about half an hour word got round the camp that they had given in. An officer came to see them. They stopped work immediately. An infuriated sergeant punched Alfred and poured a bucket of water over him.

That evening, the men were all back together in the guardroom. None of them had given up.

Throughout this story, there are many instances of hardship and cruelty, but there were also many times when the men experienced small acts of kindness. That evening, sitting in the guardroom, Alfred was to benefit from one of them.

A soldier sent his dinner to him, with his compliments. Alfred was amazed by this, and very grateful not just for the food but the kindness. He sent his thanks back to the soldier through one of the guards, but never found out who had given up his supper.

Howard found some of the officers to be reasonable men.

'There was a little Scottish sergeant-major, and he almost had tears in his eyes...he said, "You don't know what you're up against. You'll have an awful time." And he was really genuinely concerned at the trouble that we were going to meet.'

One evening, the sergeant of the Irish Guards looked in on the men in the guardroom. Alfred was taken aback at what he had to say. He asked the men if they had any money. They replied that they had a bit, though not very much. Then the sergeant explained that all the officers had gone into Le Havre for the evening, and wondered if Alfred and the others would like to have a party of their own. He took what little money they had, and a while later brought back an enormous spread of decent food, which their own money could never have paid for by itself.

The evening ended with singing, with the sergeant himself taking the lead, while the men hummed an accompaniment. They sang a memorial song, written about the life of an Irish patriot who had been executed in 1803 for his part in an attempted uprising against the British. The song contains the lines:

*Hung, drawn and quartered, sure that was
my sentence,
But soon I will show them no cow'rd am I.*

*My crime is the love of the land I was
 born in,
A hero I lived and a hero I'll die.*

These words were about a man of a very
different kind from Alfred and Howard, but
nonetheless it must have been a stirring
moment.

The men continued their battle of wills at
Cinder City Camp. Many of them were given
Field Punishment Number One. Howard was
tied up for three nights out of four, for two
hours at a time. Some of the others were sent
to a Field Punishment Unit at nearby
Harfleur, where they were tied to a wooden
framework. They were tied to upright posts,
with their arms outstretched along horizontal
beams, and their faces pressed against barbed
wire. After several hours, the tightness of the
ropes became extremely painful, and for men

of less than average height, the effort of standing on tiptoes to relieve the weight of their bodies was severe. This was the punishment known, for obvious reasons, as 'crucifixion'.

The army also continued to try and use more psychological methods to break the men. Howard knew that they weren't empty threats.

'We were forever being threatened with the death sentence. Over and over again we'd be marched up and read out a notice: some man being sentenced to death through disobedience at the front. They had the power to.'

Although it seems extraordinary to us now, many soldiers were indeed shot by their own army for reasons such as desertion, disobedience or cowardice. Many of these were official executions after court martial, but there were other less formal cases in the trenches. It was not uncommon, when an order to attack had been given, for an officer to have to shoot one of his men to make the others go 'over the top' into the German gunfire.

When Robert Graves arrived for the first time in Le Havre, in May 1915 – a year before Alfred and Howard got there – he read the back files of army orders at the rest camp. At least twenty men had been shot for cowardice. Yet just a few days later in Parliament, the minister responsible assured the House of Commons that no death sentences had been carried out.

Alfred and Howard and the others continued to refuse to obey orders and showed no sign of weakening. In an attempt to break the stalemate, the army decided to up the stakes again. This would take the men to the edge of death.

CHAPTER 9

THE AREA
OF DEATH

IT WAS DECIDED to send the men not to the actual front line, but to Boulogne. However, Boulogne was technically in the 'field zone', the front line area. This meant that disobedience could now be punished -by death.

They were loaded aboard a windowless railway truck, bearing the words, '40 hommes – 8 chevaux,' that is '40 men – 8 horses.'

They struggled to light some candles, but soon gave up and sat in darkness on piles of kit bags and boxes. The journey was incredibly slow; it took two days to travel 150 miles. The heavily loaded train travelled very slowly and stopped many times on the way.

At Rouen, the door of their truck slid back to reveal an awesome spectacle, which made a great impression on Alfred. Adjoining the platform was a vast warehouse. It was filled with thousands of men, all awaiting their various orders: wounded men going home; a few lucky ones joining them for leave in 'Blighty'; and many more headed for the trenches.

At this time British High Command was gearing up for the huge offensive known as the Battle of the Somme, which would ultimately result in the death and wounding of over 1.2 million men.

At Boulogne, the men were marched straight away to a disused fish market, which was being used as a Field Punishment Barracks. No time was lost. The seventeen conscientious objectors and other prisoners were paraded out in two lines, and then ordered to 'double-up'. This meant they had to run around the compound. One of the guards called out a couple of Scots to lead the men around, and told them to set a fast pace.

About three-quarters of the way round on the first lap, Howard suddenly called to the others. Without realizing it, they had obeyed an order. Howard pointed this out and immediately all seventeen men stopped dead in their tracks. At once there was uproar from the guards and the other men. Alfred saw one of the warders, known as 'Old Dartmoor' after the well-known English prison in Devon, reach for his revolver, as did the other guards.

The Unit's commander, Colour-Sergeant Barber was called out. Amid much shouting, he yelled, 'Tie 'em up!'

Immediately they were taken away. They received another dose of 'crucifixion', this time with the horizontal ropes holding their wrists high above their heads, making the punishment more painful. They were left like this for four hours.

It would not be the last time the men were tied up at the Field Punishment Unit. Indeed, it was a nightly occurrence until a new way of dealing with them was introduced. They were put in irons, with their hands behind their backs, and placed in an underground cage.

The cage was a heavy timber structure, essentially a cell, which had been buried under the ground. It could only be reached by a passage from above, and the only light was what filtered down from the opening. The

cage measured 11 feet 9 inches by 11 feet
3 inches (just under four square metres).
Into this space were placed seventeen men,
with one bucket, with no lid, to use as a
latrine.

The men were to spend many days in this
cage, handcuffed except when being
interviewed by an officer. The only change in
the routine came at night, when the handcuffs
were fastened in front of them so they could
sleep. They were fed four hard biscuits and
eight ounces (200g) of corned beef a day, and
had to drink heavily chlorinated water.

Even in this hole, the men were still able
to laugh. Going to the toilet, with hands in
irons behind their backs, caused them some
problems. They had to work together to
undo a man's trousers and do them back up
again afterwards, and the antics that resulted
from this often caused them much
amusement.

After three days they managed to get their handcuffs removed, and things became a little easier.

Howard was separated from the others, having been identified as a ringleader. He sat in a cell next to the others, but was able to speak to them through gaps in the planks.

On Sunday morning, they were let out so they could wash, and after dinner that evening all the prisoners were drawn up in the compound to hear the announcement of a death sentence passed a few days before on a soldier found guilty of disobedience.

The men needed no further reminder of the seriousness of their situation, and it was around this time that rumours started to spread that they were soon to be tried by a Field General Court Martial, which would have life or death powers over them.

When Howard heard these rumours, he immediately applied for permission to send a telegram to London, to get legal representation at his trial. He wrote a draft of the message he wanted telegraphed to England. But he was to be disappointed: a few hours later his letter was returned and he was told that permission to send the telegram had been denied by the base commandant. Howard was amazed that Colonel Wilberforce, who would be the principal witness for the prosecution at his court martial, had the power to prevent the defendant from obtaining legal help.

Things looked bleak, but by another stroke of luck, word at last reached the No-Conscription Fellowship, back in London, of the men's whereabouts. Soldiers in the First World War were given army regulation postcards to send home, with fixed wording already printed on them. One of another group of conscientious objectors who had now joined the others was John Brocklesby. He had managed to cross out various letters in the words on the postcard so that what was left read, 'I'm being sent to B ou long'. Incredibly, it passed the censor and as a result of this, the No-Conscription Fellowship took immediate action. Questions were asked in Parliament by MPs sympathetic to the men's cause. Like the letter thrown from the train window, this proved to be another turning point.

After a couple of weeks in the cage, Alfred became ill. He went down with dysentery, a disease common where sanitation is poor. Now his story was to run a slightly different course from that of the others, for he was removed from the Field Punishment Unit and taken under guard to Number 13 Stationary Hospital in Boulogne. After fourteen days in the hospital he was taken to a nearby army camp in the countryside and placed in a guard tent. The weather was good and the surroundings beautiful, but things were grim for Alfred.

No sooner had he arrived at the camp than one of the guards came and spoke to him.

'You're in for it,' said the guard, 'Your lot's been shot.'

CHAPTER 10

THE DEATH
SENTENCE

THE NO-CONSCRIPTION Fellowship was
undergoing court cases of its own back
in Britain at the same time the conscientious
objectors in France were facing their courts
martial. Nonetheless, as soon as they had con-
firmation of the men's location they managed
to organise some help. Questions over the
treatment and whereabouts of the men were
asked in the House of Commons. As a result

two people, the Reverend F.B. Meyer, and Hubert Peet, a Quaker journalist, managed to get permission to visit the men in France to report on their condition.

The visitors were taken on a tour of the Field Punishment Unit, but were not shown the underground cage. Some of the men were allowed to speak to the visitors, in the presence of guards, and explained their position on war and the basis of their objection to fighting.

The men were returned to their cell to await events. They passed the time as they had before: playing guessing games; holding debates; sleeping much of the time. Howard remembers how it felt.

'Even during the daytime we slept a great deal, and, in the wooden cage, one felt a strange resemblance to an animal in captivity, pacing up and down before meals and after "feeding time" lying down to rest.'

Things were coming to a head, however.
On the morning of 2nd June, Howard and
three of the others, Jack Foister, John Ring
and Harry Scullard, who were also regarded
as ringleaders, were marched to the courtroom
with an escort carrying rifles with fixed
bayonets.

Howard was led into the court and his
court martial began, in a small building in the
camp that was little more than a hut.
Nevertheless it was an intimidating affair.
Both sides knew the seriousness of Howard's
crimes and of the possible punishments.
There were three members of the court: a
major and two officers of lesser rank.

As Howard made his statement the court
was still and silent, and he felt he was given
a fair hearing. Howard sensed that at least
one of the men found the whole situation very
uncomfortable, an opinion reinforced by
something he discovered later. Outside, one of

his companions overheard an officer remark that 'it would be monstrous to shoot these men.'

Howard nervously left the court martial to await sentencing, which would follow in a few days. However, this was all to prove a waste of time. It seemed there had been a technical mistake in the hearing, apparently because the officer who had heard the case was of inferior rank to the principal witness, the base commandant. Howard was not sure, though.

'I was much more inclined to think myself that the first court martial hadn't given a stiff enough sentence or verdict, and that they wanted something more, but anyway we had to go through the whole business all over again.'

So, on 7th June they came before the court for a second time, and the whole procedure

was performed again, with no detail omitted.
It took almost all day to hear the cases of
Howard and the other three men. Howard
felt a different attitude towards him this time.

*'I did sense that the second court martial
was much more hostile. I could sort of pick
up their attitude. It must have been very
annoying to the Base Commandant who
had to come down from his office in each
case to give evidence. The poor, wretched
man must have been thoroughly fed up
with this business.'*

Just over a week later the end of the ordeal
had come.

On the evening of Thursday 15th June
1916, Howard and his three companions
were escorted by military police to the
Henriville Camp, in order for their sentences
to be read out.

Once again it was an impressive affair, with the Non-Combatant Corps and labour battalions drawn up on three sides of the parade ground. The fourth side of the square was taken by the men and their escort.

A great hum of whispered conversation ran round the square. At last the officers managed to silence the crowd, and Howard was marched out a few paces in front of the others. This was it. Their lives hung upon the outcome of Howard's case. Since he was the first, his was a test of what was in store for them all.

An officer read out a statement of Howard's offences: refusing to obey the orders of an officer while under active service conditions; disobedience; and so on and on. It was a long list. Then the officer announced: 'The sentence of the court is to suffer death by being shot.'

There was a pause, during which Howard simply thought, 'Well, that's that.' He felt disembodied, as if he were watching this happen to someone else. But the officer had not finished yet: 'Confirmed by the Commander in Chief, Sir Douglas Haig.' Again there was a suitable pause, and then the officer concluded the statement. 'But subsequently commuted to penal servitude for ten years.'

Howard would not be shot after all, but would be sent to prison, to serve hard labour.

Just over three months since the start of their fight, it was finished, in a way.

CHAPTER 11

AND THEN ...

MEANWHILE, ALFRED was also about to undergo court martial in Boulogne. This was a difficult time. He tried to keep going by himself, and avoided thinking about relatives and home too much, since he knew he would 'crumple up' if he did.

At his trial a captain on the bench was drunk and abusive, and the colonel presiding in the case had to tell him to be quiet. One of the sergeants presenting evidence against him bungled his statement badly. Alfred found the man unintentionally funny, and with his usual irrepressible goodwill offered to help him give evidence. Alfred was told in no uncertain terms not to interfere with the business of the court.

The result was the same as Howard's. He was found guilty, and a few days later went through the same performance of being sentenced to death, but then having the sentence commuted to penal servitude. Even in the face of death, Alfred was defiant. When ordered to step out two paces to hear his sentence, he didn't budge. He had to be pushed forward a pace or two to keep the attending officers happy. What can it feel like to hear a death sentence read out against you? Alfred remembered it clearly.

'The whole situation dies on you. You have a feeling you are no longer a part of this world, and therefore you must brace

yourself to meet the end. And that's how I think it was. I didn't show any emotion of any sort. I didn't move a muscle, I didn't smile, I didn't cry, I didn't do anything. I just stood there.'

Between his court martial and the sentence, Alfred spent some time in a Royal Army Medical Corps Decontamination Unit. All the men were being inoculated against various diseases. Alfred refused the inoculation. The captain of the Unit, a Canadian, came to see him, and asked the guard who he was. 'Conscientious objector, Sir,' said the guard. The captain turned to Alfred. 'Don't tell me you have a conscientious objection to being inoculated, too?' Alfred told him that the only healthy member of his family was the one who hadn't been inoculated. 'You know,' said the captain, 'I can make you have this.' Alfred smiled and said, 'I know you can, Sir, but you wouldn't pull a dirty trick like that on a fellow, would you?' The captain laughed, and let him be.

A couple of days later as the Unit drove away, Alfred saw the captain on the back of a truck. The captain saluted him, and Alfred just remembered in time not to salute back. Instead he raised his cap and waved.

The sentence of penal servitude meant the men would be returned to England to a civil prison, not a military one. It seemed to Howard that the army had realised that as long as the men were in military control, they would only go on offending. The only other option was to have them executed, but it seems that the visit organised by the Reverend Meyer and Hubert Peet had convinced the government that it was impossible to hand out this punishment and escape public attention. The government backed down and put the men into the civilian prison system.

If Howard had won a major battle, he felt little joy. Before him was the prospect of ten years' penal servitude in a grim prison, such as Dartmoor. Still, there was no denying the sudden disappearance of the tension that had been dogging the men for months, as they reached England.

Alfred remembers bitterly No.1 Military Prison, Rouen, a hard labour camp where he was taken next. On the way there he was treated to two first-rate meals by a kindly sergeant. This was the end of July; he had not eaten a decent meal since 25th April.

Alfred and the sergeant found that their politics agreed somewhat, but the sergeant knew his duty, and within a couple of days Alfred entered the prison at Rouen. He was ordered to perform 'shot drill', which involved picking up and putting down a heavy bag of lead, after carrying it a few

metres. This continued for several hours.
Defiant to the last, Alfred told the attending
sergeant that he did not do military drill, and
though he was set about with a stick, he
maintained his position. He was marched
back to his cell.

*'I had won. A few days later I was on my
way up the Seine from Rouen to Le Havre,
on a summer evening in a wonderful light,
through a landscape of surpassing beauty.
Next day, I was at Winchester jail to begin
ten years' penal servitude.'*

It was at Winchester that Alfred met
Howard and the others again. Until this point
he had believed they were dead.

Most of the men were released from prison
around April 1919, but lost the right to vote
for ten years. Many found it hard to get a job
because they had been conscientious

objectors. The horror of the war had not changed many people's attitudes to these men and they were still regarded as shirkers and cowards. Alfred eventually found a job, but only by moving away from London. He became a piano tuner. Howard, too, was able to return eventually to his career in banking, though before this he spent some time working for the War Victims' Relief Committee. This was an organisation created to help the victims of war in the war zone itself; in this case, France. Howard became their assistant secretary in London, helping the committee to repair the damage done by the war: rebuilding houses; constructing hospitals; restoring clean water supplies and so on. Howard received the French Red Cross for his work with the War Victims' Relief Committee, something he found a little ironic in view of his experiences.

CHAPTER 12

CONSEQUENCES

BOTH HOWARD AND ALFRED lived to be old men. The memory of those months in 1916 never left them, however. Howard kept a huge collection of photographs related to his experiences and those of men like him. Alfred found his story inspired various people interested in the peace movement over the years. As old men, Howard and Alfred and many other conscientious objectors were interviewed for the Imperial War Museum about the experiences they had been through.

At the very end of Alfred's tape, after many hours of talking, he ended his interview simply:

   'Well, that's my story. I wonder what you'll think of it.'

His words, captured on tape, have the power to keep asking this question on through the years. What do you make of his and Howard's stories? What would you have done in their place? Were they cowards or heroes?

On this last point, Alfred himself was clear. In the 1960s Associated Television made a programme about 'The Frenchmen', as they became known. The makers of the programme called it *The Saints go Marching In*. Alfred objected to this.

   'We were no saints. We were as ordinary a lot as you could meet.'

War is a confusing business, and many people have changed their minds about the issues involved. At the outbreak of the war Alfred was willing to work for the Royal Army Medical Corps. During the time before his court martial he shared a cell with a Royal Army Medical Corps man who had committed some offence. Alfred told him that he had been prepared to join the Royal Army Medical Corps, because it seemed to be humane work. The soldier replied, 'You poor fool! You don't suppose the Royal Army Medical Corps exists for humane reasons do you? They are there to ensure the fighting unit is kept up to strength and made efficient.' He told Alfred his orders were that if he saw a man who was unlikely to make a reasonable recovery, he was just to give him a morphine injection to dull the pain, and move on to the next man. Alfred changed his mind about Royal Army Medical Corps work after that.

All sorts of stories emerged from the war.
Robert Graves was just one of many soldiers
who had been enthusiastic volunteers at the
start of the war, only to have that belief
ground out of them by the sheer horror of it
all. Another famous poet, Siegfried Sassoon,
had been keen to fight, and had won the
Military Cross. But towards the end of the
war he had grown disillusioned, and had
thrown his medal into the sea. Shortly after
the war he spoke as a Pacifist at a General
Election rally in Brighton.

Even Winston Churchill, who played such a
key role in World War Two, and who was
First Lord of the Admiralty in World War
One, later said of the first conflict, 'There
never was so unnecessary a war.'

On the other hand, there were many
conscientious objectors from the First World
War who decided to fight in World War Two.

Some of them saw Hitler's intentions as being an entirely different thing from the old wrestling empires of World War One. In retrospect, the evidence of the holocaust reinforced this view. Some simply changed their minds about the principle of what they had done.

Many military men were unrepentant. Lieutenant Colonel Reginald Brooke, commanding officer at Wandsworth Military Detention Barracks was court-martialled as a result of his treatment of conscientious objectors. Lt. Colonel Brooke's court martial was a catalogue of unbelievable treatment of conscientious objectors in his care, with beatings, confinement and force-feeding regularly being accompanied by threatening language.

Lt. Colonel Brooke was said to have been delighted to hear of the treatment of Alfred

and Howard and the other men sent to
France. He said he hoped, '… the whole lot of
the conscientious objectors would be treated
in the same way', that he cared nothing for
Parliament, and that he would do exactly as
he liked with these men.

> *'I shall continue to act in my barracks*
> *according to my orders, without any regard*
> *for what you or any of the so-called 'public'*
> *may think. I do not care one atom for*
> *public opinion.'*

Lt. Colonel Brooke was dismissed.

And what, if anything was the result of
their protest? On 25th May 1916, Army
Order X was issued, under which offenders
passed from court martial into civil prisons,
thus removing the problem for the army.
The protests of Alfred, Howard and the

growing number of conscientious objectors had undoubtedly sped this decision along. The one thing the army didn't need was a band of rebels to act as martyrs, which might provoke further unrest amongst the conscripted soldiers.

In all, 16,500 men registered a conscientious objection to the war. What happened to them varied enormously. 1200 conscientious objectors served with the Friends Ambulance Unit, a Quaker organisation independent of the military. Fifty or so received death sentences, subsequently commuted. Many ended up in hospital as a result of their treatment in prison. It is known that at least ten were not so lucky and died there. Thirty-one are known to have suffered severe psychiatric illness.

The accounts of the treatment of conscientious objectors inside the country's

jails led to prison reforms not long after
the war.

Furthermore, the actions of these men in the
face of the introduction of conscription paved
the way for conscientious objectors in World
War Two, when over 60,000 men registered
as such. Their path was a much easier one,
because men like Howard and Alfred had
established an individual's right to hold such a
belief. And certainly, the protests of men like
Alfred and Howard, and the work of the
No-Conscription Fellowship defeated the
army's original intention to shoot those who
refused to fight.

Alfred never doubted that he had done the
right thing, though he did later sometimes
wonder what it had achieved. However, he
felt that progress often comes about from
people doing unorthodox things, against the
mass of popular opinion.

There are some acts, some statements of belief that are hard to criticise. The story of Howard Marten and Alfred Evans, though horrific in places, is no worse than those of many of the other conscientious objectors in World War One. But the story of 'The Frenchmen' is certainly remarkable, not least for the strength of their beliefs.

Here is evidence of that strength.

A day or two before Alfred's court martial a captain came to see him, and told him he had just been reviewing Alfred's papers at the company office. He told Alfred that the papers were marked DEATH in red at the top. Then he asked Alfred if he intended to go on. Alfred said, 'Yes.'

'You see, Sir, men are dying in agony in the trenches for the things they believe in, and I wouldn't be any the less than them.'

To Alfred's utter astonishment, the captain stepped back a couple of paces and saluted him. Then he came forward, extending his hand. Alfred shook it heartily. He never saw the man again.

Timeline

1914	*August*	– German Declaration of War on Russia and France
		– German invasion of Belgium
		– British Declaration of War on Germany
	Autumn	– First Battle of Ypres

1915	*Spring*	– Battle of Neuve Chapelle
	Spring	– Second Battle of Ypres
	July	– The National Registration Act comes into force

1916	*Spring*	– Battle of Verdun
	March	– The Military Service Act comes into force
	March	– Howard and Alfred appear before their tribunals
	April	– The men are sent to the Harwich Redoubt
	7th May	– The men are shipped to France
	2nd June	– The death sentence is passed on Alfred and Howard
		– The men return to Britain
	Summer –Autumn	– Battle of the Somme

| 1918 | *November* | – Ceasefire |

Glossary

COMMUTED: when a serious sentence, such as the death penalty, is reduced to a lesser one, it is said to have been commuted.

CONSCIENTIOUS OBJECTOR: one who refuses to serve in the army despite being conscripted to do so, usually for moral or religious reasons.

CONSCRIPT: a person forced by law to join the armed forces whether they want to or not.

DEFENDANT: someone accused of a crime is called the defendant at their trial in court.

DERBY SCHEME: introduced in late 1915, this government scheme put pressure on men to 'attest' – to say that they would serve in the army when called upon to do so.

FIELD PUNISHMENT NUMBER ONE: an army term describing a variety of physical punishments, some of which were extremely brutal.

Glossary

FRIENDS AMBULANCE UNIT: a Quaker organisation, which provided ambulance and medical services in the war zone.

FRONT LINE: the foremost position to which an army has advanced.

LATRINE: a toilet in a camp or barracks, often fairly primitive.

MILTARY SERVICE ACT – MARCH 1916: the first Act of Conscription introduced in the United Kingdom.

NATIONAL REGISTRATION ACT – JULY 1915: this Act of Parliament compelled all men between 16 and 40 to register. It was a forerunner to the Military Service Act of 1916.

NO-CONSCRIPTION FELLOWSHIP: an organisation established by those sympathetic to conscientious objectors to provide support and information.

NON-COMBATANT CORPS: a section of the army established by the government as an alternative to the regular army. It was intended conscientious objectors would be happy to serve in this Corps, since they did not actually fight.

NO-MAN'S-LAND: the area between the front lines of two armies, controlled by neither side.

PACIFIST: a person who believes that disputes should be resolved by peaceful means, and who rejects the use of violence and war.

PARLIAMENTARY RECRUITING SERVICE: a government organisation whose role was to oversee all aspects of recruitment into the army.

PENAL SERVITUDE: imprisonment with hard labour.

QUAKERS: the short name for the Religious Society of Friends – a Christian movement that upholds strong principles of peace and rejects formal systems of worship.

ROYAL ARMY MEDICAL CORPS: the army's ambulance and hospital service.

SOCIALISM: political theory advocating that society should be run on a constructive basis founded on equality, rather than a competitive one, as in capitalism.

TRADE UNION: an organisation of workers in a trade or industry that exists to protect their rights and welfare.

TRIBUNAL: a court of justice.

Index

Index

About the author

Marcus Sedgwick has been a teacher, a bookseller and now works in publishing. He is also a wood and stone carver and wood engraver. He lives in West Sussex and has a young daughter.

Marcus won the Branford Boase Award for the best debut children's novel in 2000, for *Floodland*. This was followed by two more books for children, *Witch Hill* and *The Dark Horse*. .

Cowards is one of Hodder Children's Books' literary non fiction books, about real people who do extraordinary things.